GW00631120

lela...

From:

Cis, with love

Date:

12 : 04 : 2015.

Raindrops from Heaven

Published by Christian Art Publishers
PO Box 1599, Vereeniging, 1930, RSA

© 2013
First edition 2013

Designed by Christian Art Publishers

Images used under license from Shutterstock.com

Printed in China

ISBN 978-1-4321-0678-2

13 14 15 16 17 18 19 20 21 22 – 10 9 8 7 6 5 4 3 2 1

RAINDROPS

FROM *Heaven*

CHRISTIAN ART
PUBLISHERS

Kind words

are like a gentle
shower of rain.
The softer it
falls, the longer
it dwells upon and
the deeper it sinks
into the mind.

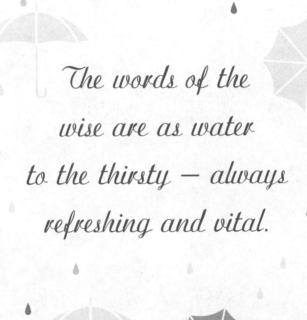

The words of the
wise are as water
to the thirsty — always
refreshing and vital.

Faith

in God gives you a

front-row seat

to a life

of *miracles*.

"Don't be afraid.
Just have faith."

Mark 5:36

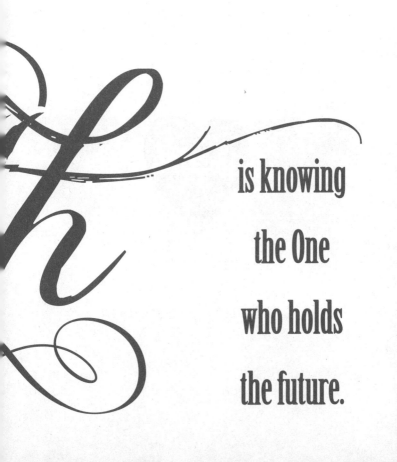

h is knowing
the One
who holds
the future.

God listens to our

more than

to our words.

Faith in God

helps us move

mountains

of impossibilities

by moving

a stone at a time.

gratitude dispels the

clouds of a gloomy day.

A true friend
is one
who steps
to the
foreground
when trouble
sets in.

A friend loves at all times.

Prov. 17:17

If you cannot

take care

of minor

things, you're

not **worthy**

to major.

Never forget to make
time to *enjoy*
the small things!

See
the day
of small things
as a door to
great
opportunities.

The Lord will indeed give what is good.

Ps. 85:12

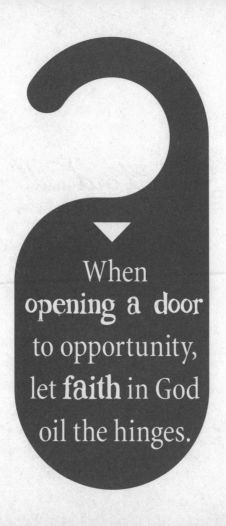

When
opening a door
to opportunity,
let **faith** in God
oil the hinges.

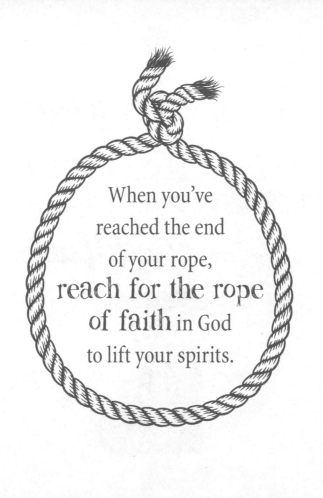

When you've
reached the end
of your rope,
reach for the rope
of faith in God
to lift your spirits.

The God of all *grace*
will Himself restore you
and make you strong,
firm and *steadfast.*

1 Pet. 5:10

Faith

in God is not an
escape route
from the pain of life.
It's a divine gift
of inner strength
to enable you to conquer
the storms of life
courageously.

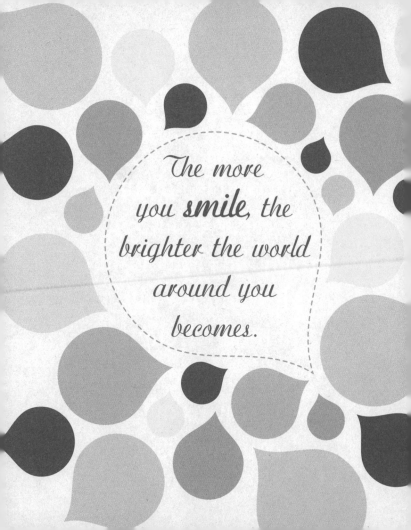

The more you **smile**, the brighter the world around you becomes.

Faith is the
confidence that
what we hope for
will actually
happen; it gives us
assurance about
things we
cannot see.

Heb. 11:1

Faith in God

is to set the sails of your lifeboat

to reach your destination

regardless of the direction

of the wind.

The LORD is my
light and my *salvation* –
whom shall I fear?
The LORD is the
stronghold of my life –
of whom shall I be afraid?

Ps. 27:1

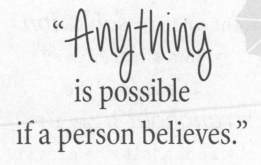

"Anything
is possible
if a person believes."

Mark 9:23

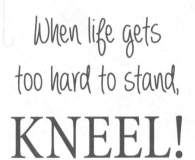

When life gets
too hard to stand,

KNEEL!

yer

is without

a price but priceless

in rewards.

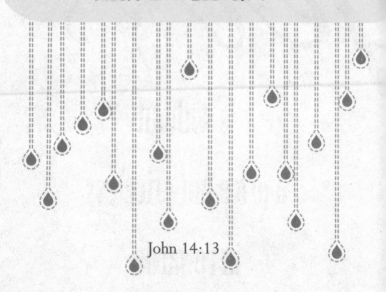

"Whatever you ask
in My name,
that I will do."

John 14:13

Guidance

in troublesome times
is only a kneel away.

As a
flashlight,
when you're lost in the night,

helps you to keep on track

and find your way safely back,

so is a

prayer
when you feel perplexed

in your plight.

The prayer
of a righteous person
is powerful and effective.

James 5:16

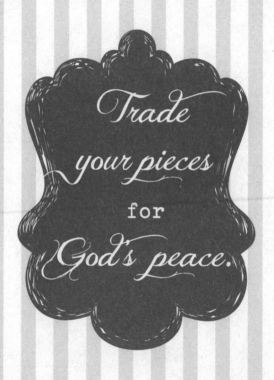

Trade your pieces for God's peace.

To,
by *prayer,*
find yourself
in the center
of God's

heart

is to find
peace and
serenity,
the storms
to outlast.

God, who gives hope,
is watching over you
and gives you peace
as you put your trust in Him.

Peace
and
mercy
to all who follow
His rule.

Gal. 6:16

A **grudge harbored in the heart** is a thief robbing you

of your most precious possession –

 peace of mind.

Giving others
a piece of your mind
is a sure way
of losing
peace of mind.

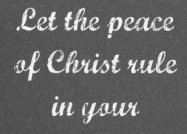

Let the peace
of Christ rule
in your

hearts

Col. 3:15

Those who plot evil
dig a hole for themselves
to be buried in,
but those who plan good
for their fellow man
inherit peace of mind.

Joy is nectar to the soul.

One small deed of
kindness
today is a seed planted
to reap
a bountiful harvest of
joy tomorrow.

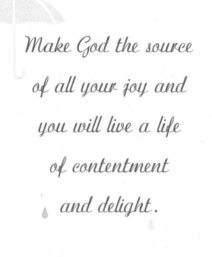

Make God the source
of all your joy and
you will live a life
of contentment
and delight.

Rejoice always.

1 Thess. 5:16

The joy of the Lord
is the music that
brightens up your
life and lightens
the load.

Joy makes
the spirit
glow longer.

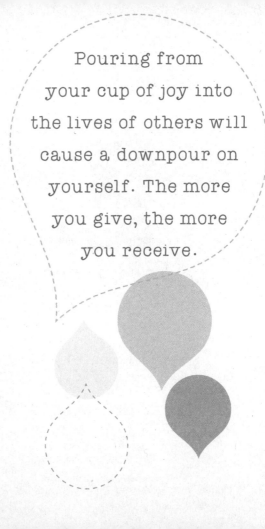

Pouring from
your cup of joy into
the lives of others will
cause a downpour on
yourself. The more
you give, the more
you receive.

My heart rejoices
in the LORD.

1 Sam. 2:1

Real joy
is the feeling
of peace within,
even amidst the storms
of life.

Real joy

does not depend on circumstances –

it flows from a

heart

filled with gratitude;

a positive and confident outlook

on life based upon faith

in God and hope for

tomorrow against all odds.

There is more

joy

in making others happy

than in waiting for others

to make you happy.

The Lord is my strength
and my song.

Ps. 118:14

Life's truest happiness
is found in friendships we make
along the way.

A friend

is someone you can depend on
to keep you on your feet
when your legs have forgotten
how to walk.

Friendship

is built on what you present -

not on what you pretend.

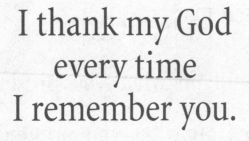

I thank my God
every time
I remember you.

Phil. 1:3

A heartened heart,
empathetic ears
and a soft tongue
build *friendships*
that will hearten the soul.

Friendship is
founded not in what
you pretend to be,
but in the way you
are prepared to share
yourself with me.

Proving a
point
for the sake
of winning
an argument
may boost
your ego,
but boots
your friends.

riend

is he whose words fall softly
on my ears, even in disagreement.

Two are
better than one,
because they have
a good reward for their labor.

Eccles. 4:9

The small things of today
attended wisely to,
become the big things
of tomorrow.

Do not despise the day of

small things.

A marathon is won
not in leaps and bounds,
but stride by stride.

Be joyful in hope,
patient in affliction,
faithful in prayer.

Rom. 12:12

If you humble yourself
to attend to small things
as if they were big things,
you'll become big enough
to do big things
in a big way.

You, Lord,

are a *compassionate*

and gracious God.

Ps. 86:15

Faith

is not believing that God can,

it is knowing that God will.

God specializes in
the impossible,
but He can do for us
only that which we,
by *faith*, allow Him to.

The LORD has done great things for us, and we are filled with *joy*.

Ps. 126:3

When you fail,
think of the many times
you've succeeded and
refuse to be discouraged.
Rather be challenged
to try again with
more experience.

May the words of

my mouth and the meditation

of my heart be pleasing

in Your sight, O LORD.

Ps. 19:14

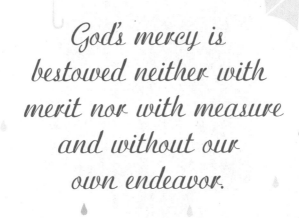

God's mercy is
bestowed neither with
merit nor with measure
and without our
own endeavor.

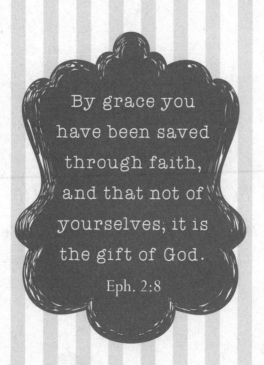

By grace you have been saved through faith, and that not of yourselves; it is the gift of God.

Eph. 2:8

Counting your
God-given
blessings will
lift your spirit
more than
counting your
earthly possessions.

Keep me

as the apple of Your eye;
hide me in the shadow
of Your wings.

Ps. 17:8

For He is a God of
compassion
who deals with you
kindly;
taking care of you
every step of the way
on your *journey*,
daily and nightly.

God didn't promise to give us answers to life's problems, only directions if we put our trust in Him.

You, O Lᴏʀᴅ, are a compassionate and gracious God, slow to anger, abounding in love and faithfulness.

Ps. 86:15

Look at yourself
for what you will be,
not what you
are now —

God does!

The LORD directs
the steps of the godly.
He **delights** in every
detail of their lives.

Ps. 37:23

Treasure a good
relationship as
if it was a
precious gem.

Let us fix our eyes
on **Jesus,** the author
and **perfecter** of our
faith, who for the **joy**
set before Him
endured the **cross.**

Heb. 12:2

Don't get upset when others don't understand you. First show **respect** by **trying** to understand them and likewise you will be respected and understood.

Show proper respect to

everyone, love the family of

believers, fear God.

1 Pet. 2:17

When at odds,
do not determine
who is right,
but what is right to keep
relationships undefiled.

Conflicts well managed

can lead to inner-life growth

and *strengthening*

of relationships.

A relationship is like a garden; it constantly needs nurturing.

Glory, honor and peace for everyone who does good.

Rom. 2:10

Blessings of gratitude

Mastering the art of gratitude is an antidote to grudges nestling in your heart.

*Preserve cherished
memories in a jar
of gratitude to refresh
your soul in times
of dryness.*

Stop searching for happiness and start making it happen by creating a heart of gratitude.

*Gloom departs
when
gratitude starts.*

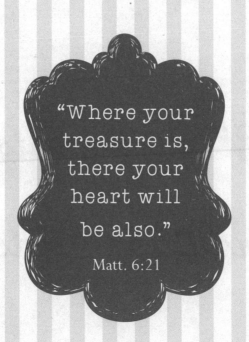

"Where your
treasure is,
there your
heart will
be also."

Matt. 6:21

Treasure
your blessings
more than
you cherish
your earthly
possessions.

Worship the LORD with gladness;
come before Him with joyful songs.

Ps. 100:2

Utilize all your senses
to *enjoy* the gift of
life fully. Hear the wind
rustling through the trees;
look at a *beautiful* flower,
the sunrise or sunset;
smell the fresh air early
in the morning; taste the
freshness of water and
thank God that you're alive.

What a gift!

Develop a positive attitude
by overlooking at least two
negative things today and
thanking God for not less
than two blessings
He sent your way.

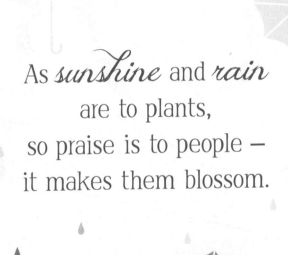

As *sunshine* and *rain*
are to plants,
so praise is to people —
it makes them blossom.

In Him our **hearts** rejoice,
for we **trust** in His holy name.

Ps. 33:21

Praise is seed
you sow in the lives of
others as well as your
own for inner growth.

He who **praises** others has
a rich storehouse of gifts
to make them and
himself happy.

Raindrops from heaven

Encouraging words
are as gentle
as the springtime rains
upon the earth.

Look for something
good in others to praise
them for and it will
open your eyes to
become aware of
more good than
bad around you.

Smile!

A bright smile to give
the world today brings
happiness all along the way.

You fill me with joy

in Your presence,

O Lord.

Ps. 16:11

The right word at the right time,

oh, what glee!

Like mercy from above

it drops gently into the heart,

meeting our every plea.